CONTENTS

G000241551

Poetry Book Society

CHOICE SELECTORS RECOMMENDATION SPECIAL COMMENDATION	SANDEEP PARMAR & TIM LIARDET
TRANSLATION SELECTOR	GEORGE SZIRTES
PAMPHLET SELECTORS	A.B. JACKSON DENISE SAUL
GUEST SELECTOR	KAYO CHINGONYI
CONTRIBUTORS	ALICE KATE MULLEN NATHANIEL SPAIN EMILY TATE REBECCA ROBINSON SOPHIE O'NEILL
EDITORIAL & DESIGN	ALICE KATE MULLEN

Membership Options
Associate - *4 bulletins a year* (UK £18, Europe £20, Overseas £23)
Full - *4 books and 4 bulletins a year* (£55, £65, £75)
Charter - *20 books and 4 bulletins* (£170, £185, £215)
Education - *4 books, 4 bulletins and teaching notes* (£58, £68, £78)
Charter Education - *20 books, 4 bulletins and teaching notes* (£180, £195, £225)
Translation - *4 Recommended translations and 4 bulletins* (£70, £100, £118)
Student - *4 books and 4 bulletins* (£27, £47, £57)
Single copies £5
Subscribe at www.poetrybooks.co.uk
Cover artwork by Jo Hume www.johume.co.uk
Copyright Poetry Book Society and contributors. All rights reserved.
ISBN 978-1-9998589-1-9 ISSN 0551-1690

Supported using public funding by
ARTS COUNCIL ENGLAND

Poetry Book Society | Inpress Books | Churchill House | 12 Mosley Street |
Newcastle upon Tyne | NE1 1DE | 0191 230 8100 | pbs@inpressbooks.co.uk

LETTER FROM THE PBS

Thank you to everyone who has been in touch with positive responses to the new-look *Bulletin*. A lot of work went into the redesign and we really appreciate your comments.

As with last quarter, I need to start this letter with a farewell and a welcome. I'd like to extend a huge thank you to Tim Liardet who has come to the end of his Selector tenure with this *Bulletin*. Tim has written some wonderful and incisive commentaries in the time we have worked together and was extremely supportive when we took over management of the PBS, we will miss him!

We are delighted to welcome Vidyan Ravinthiran as our new Book Selector. Vidyan's first collection *Grun-tu-molani*, published by Bloodaxe, was shortlisted for many awards including the Forward Prize for Best First Collection. He reviews frequently in *Poetry Review, Poetry London, PN Review* and the *TLS* and is currently a lecturer at Birmingham University.

Our events continue with the PBS sponsored StAnza lecture by Sinéad Morrissey on 8th March and Bolton University PBS Showcase featuring Karen McCarthy Woolf and Michael Symmons Roberts on the 24th April. We also look forward to welcoming you to Newcastle on the 3rd May for the Northern Poetry Symposium at Sage Gateshead. This year's symposium explores poetry in translation in partnership with NCLA and The Poettrio Experiment Project at Newcastle University. NCLA's Newcastle Poetry Festival runs from the 2nd – 5th of May, opening with US Pulitzer prize-winner and PBS Recommendation Jorie Graham. The festival programme will be launched by Jackie Kay on the 15th March.

If you missed the Vlog reviews by Jen Campbell of the PBS Winter selections, they can be found on www.poetrybooks.co.uk. The Spring Vlog will go live in March. We had some wonderful submissions to the Student Poetry Prize which will be judged by Sam Buchan-Watts. The winners will be announced in early March and the 1st prize winning poem will be featured in the Summer *Bulletin*.

We hope you enjoy our Spring Selections, we are delighted to have so many debut collections within the Choice and Recommendations this time. It is really inspiring to read so many new and varied voices.

- Sophie O'Neill, PBS and Inpress Director

SOPHIE COLLINS

Sophie Collins grew up in Bergen, North Holland, and now lives in Edinburgh. She is co-editor of *tender*, an online arts quarterly, and editor of *Currently & Emotion* (Test Centre, 2016), an anthology of contemporary poetry translations. *small white monkeys*, a text on self-expression, self-help and shame, was published by Book Works in November 2017 as part of a commissioned residency at Glasgow Women's Library. *Who Is Mary Sue?* is her first poetry collection.

WHO IS MARY SUE?

Sophie Collins Who Is Mary Sue?

Poetry   **ff**

FABER | £10.99 | PBS PRICE £8.25

The lyric subject, the "I" as an object or specimen of representation, is one of the main fields of enquiry in Sophie Collins' *Who is Mary Sue?* Who or what is the self, as embodied, gendered, subject to violence, shame and desire, in this "apparently personal" (to paraphrase Sharon Olds) space of poetry?

In her collection's title sequence, Collins addresses the many ways in which women's writing, and women authors, are denigrated. Mary Sue, we are told, is a "pejorative term" which categorises female protagonists of fan fiction as idealised versions of the author. An all-too familiar social and aesthetic combination of bad reading and misogyny devalues any writing that privileges female experience as narcissism. As Collins writes: "Thus Mary Sue becomes, in my eyes, an unwitting embodiment of the double standard of content."

From 'Preface' to 'Postface', Collins sets her sights on the author-self, as constructed by late capitalism. Her sequence, 'A Whistle in the Gloom', begins with a passage from Denise Riley's *Words as Selves* that contextualises one of Collins' central concerns: authenticity. Here, the originality of the "I" is a linguistic impossibility – it is shared, it is imperfectly self-referential, and ultimately its "grammatical offer of uniqueness is untrue". Collins invokes the pseudonymously written and famously sadomasochistic novel *Story of O* as an unidealised net for her meditation on female subjectivity. The novel's protagonist "O" becomes many things; but like the "I" it stands at the interface between being and non-being. The "O" offers an alternate space of expression – an exit, an entrance.

> Here I will purge the associations by listing them: zero (none); an exclamation (archaic); a lament (archaic); an interjection (archaic); a circle; a ring; any body orifice, including a gasping mouth or gaping anus; and, more tenuously, the grand rooms and dungeons to whose walls O is fixed; a mirror; an eye; a wound.

SANDEEP PARMAR

SOPHIE COLLINS

Who Is Mary Sue? wears many of its influences on its sleeve. The book cites Joanna Russ, Lorrie Moore, Jamaica Kincaid, Rachel Cusk and Denise Riley, among others. The tone of certain poems in the collection was definitely influenced by Clarice Lispector's translated prose – Idra Novey's translation of *The Passion According to G.H.*, in particular. Jean Rhys is mentioned in a note at the back of *Who Is Mary Sue?*; she's someone whose work has been important to me since I started writing.

Like many readers and writers I become obsessive – fannish – about the books I love. I cherish them as objects and hoard any information I can find about them. Pauline Réage's *Story of O*, the subject of one of the collection's prose pieces, is one such book. I came to Réage's novel through an essay by Canadian poet Lisa Robertson. After reading Robertson on Réage, I became fixated with *Story of O*'s narrative and its relationship to its author's life. This kind of interest in Réage is one that contradicts some of my assertions in my collection's title piece, 'Who Is Mary Sue?'. But something I've tried to explore in the book is this notion of a non-essentialist self – of the self as composed of multiple, competing selves – and I feel that the ability to harbour conflicting perspectives is evidence of this.

Of course *Story of O* is a book that many found, and continue to find, extremely shocking. This is part of its appeal for me. I think there is a sense in which dealing and / or not dealing with (i.e., repressing) trauma in my writing has meant that I've often been drawn to narratives whose female protagonists undergo a kind of incremental (self-)annihilation. My fascination with a progressive physical and psychological obliteration ended up informing parts of *Who Is Mary Sue?*'s structure and, thematically, some of its darker moments.

SOPHIE RECOMMENDS ————————————————

All of Selima Hill. But *Bunny*, especially. Everything – poetry and prose – by Denise Riley. Theory wise, I've particularly enjoyed *Impersonal Passion*, W.S. Graham and Bhanu Kapil. I seem to have reached that fabled point at which it's a challenge to find work that gets you excited about reading and writing again, but both of these poets are doing just that. I'm planning to read Graham's *New Collected Poems* over Christmas.

I CHOICE

8

SISTER

Sister, listen to me – tonight our father will pull open the heavy door of our home, walk with his large boots into the kitchen and drop a pig on the table. In the morning, peasants with children and glassy-eyed babies will enter, sniffing at us like animals, noting the absence of a mother who lays out cold plates, white bread.

SOPHIE COLLINS

POSTFACE

The author pulls some boxes from an archive.
She opens a box marked VIOLENCE AGAINST WOMEN BOX 5.
She reads a short text on the use of lemon juice as an offensive
    weapon.
The author opens a box marked VIOLENCE AGAINST WOMEN
    BOX 4.
She sifts newspaper clippings.
She takes photographs.
The author tells those who ask that she is undertaking a residency.
She tells those who show interest that she is thinking about shame.
She is asked on more than one occasion to offer a distinction
    between shame and guilt.
The author joins a copyright library.
She reads parts of Sara Ahmed's *The Cultural Politics of Emotion*.
She transcribes, *In shame, I am the object as well as the subject of
    the feeling.*

SOPHIE COLLINS

10

KAVEH AKBAR

Kaveh Akbar's poems appear in *The New Yorker*, *Poetry*, *The New York Times*, *The Guardian*, PBS Newshour, *The Poetry Review*, and elsewhere. Kaveh is the founding editor of *Divedapper*, and has received a Pushcart Prize and a Ruth Lilly and Dorothy Sargent Rosenberg Poetry Fellowship from the Poetry Foundation. He was born in Tehran, Iran, and currently lives and teaches in Indiana. *Calling a Wolf a Wolf* is his first book.

CALLING A WOLF A WOLF

PENGUIN | £9.99 | PBS PRICE £7.50

With an expansive verbal dynamism, the poems in Kaveh Akbar's *Calling a Wolf a Wolf* confront the body's own ability to survive. In a series of lyric portraits, the figure of an alcoholic wrests itself from a metaphysical thirst for annihilation. Elsewhere an impacable longing for identity, an ancestral language usurped by migration, severs the self from its context, history, home. In 'Portrait of the Alcoholic With Doubt and Kingfisher', desire – spiritual as much as bodily thirst and hunger – becomes a site of metamorphosis. These 'Portraits' are not artificial or self-conscious revelations but dialogues with receding former selves.

> Starving mice will often eat their own tails
>
> before ceding to hunger. The lesson:
> it's never too late to become
> a new thing, to rip the fur
>
> from your face and dive
> dimplefirst into the strange.

The poem 'Desunt Nonnulla', meaning 'some things are lacking', reads like a statement of insatiable poetics:

> ...if you teach me something
> beautiful   I will name it quickly before it floats away.

Where the child in Elizabeth Bishop's 'The Waiting Room' screams at the thought of her mortality, Akbar's 'Long Pig' sets its sights on the cannibal who is both self and other. This tension – held on the line almost breathlessly – between the grotesque and the sacred, survival and death, faith and knowing, is the human dilemma which the poet skilfully handles. Even when the "I" appears, the weight of its construction feels less personal than rhetorical. These poems are not confessions, but ecstatic meditations on the nature of being. Their astonishment is keenly wrought into a landscape of estrangement, violence and prayer. Throughout Akbar's work the self recurs to interrogate its maker and, in doing so, irreverently dismantles the world.

SANDEEP PARMAR

KAVEH AKBAR

The poems in *Calling a Wolf a Wolf* were little life-rafts – I'd just gotten sober, and I had no idea what to do with myself, with my physical or psychic self. My whole adult life had been spent lurching from crisis to crisis; I had no relationship to a living that wasn't predicated on the pursuit of narcotic experience. The poems became a place to put myself for hours, days, weeks in a row. Over time, one set of addictions gradually sublimated into another – I woke daily and threw myself into the haven of poetry, found it to be a vessel capable of holding my obsessiveness, my fervor. I read everything, everyone, and wrote more or less constantly. After about three years of this, three years of recovery-through-poetry, I had written the first recognizable manuscript of *Calling a Wolf a Wolf.*

In *A Year With Swollen Appendices*, Brian Eno writes, "The blues singer with the cracked voice is the sound of an emotional cry too powerful for the throat that releases it. The excitement of grainy film, of bleached-out black and white, is the excitement of witnessing events too momentous for the medium assigned to record them." In *Calling a Wolf a Wolf*, I am profoundly interested in how I might achieve this effect in poems, on the page and on the tongue and in the ear. Rilke writes about people knowing they have "death inside them like the stone inside a fruit." Writing my poems, that knowledge was so pronounced in me, the membrane between me and an early preventable death was so thin I could press my ear up to it and hear my own voice on the other side. I became fascinated by the way my poems could and could not bear the weight of that.

KAVEH RECOMMENDS

Frank Bidart's new *Collected* is a near-religious object and I treat it as such. It's one of my favorite collections of poems I've ever read, period. This year I have also thrilled through a seemingly endless stream of brilliant new poetry books, including ones by Nicole Sealey, Natalie Shapero, Nuar Alsadir, Chen Chen, Gabrielle Calvocoressi, Danez Smith, Carl Phillips, Layli Long Soldier, Alessandra Lynch, Javier Zamora, and many, many others.

I RECOMMENDATION

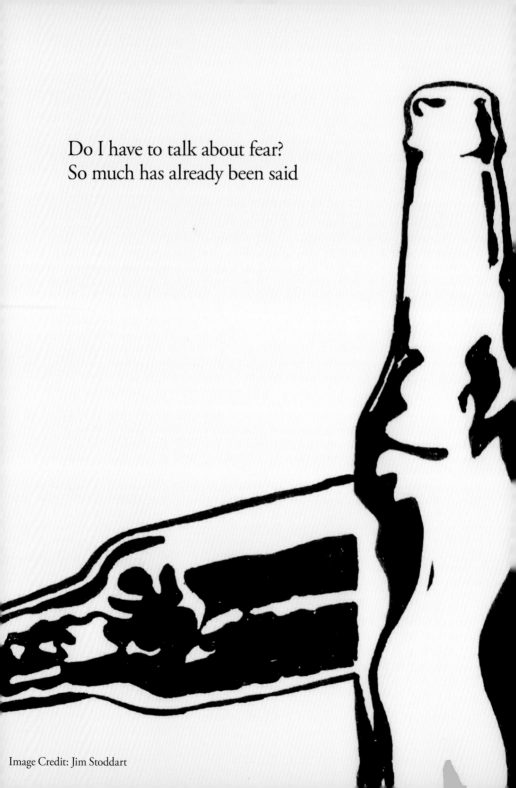

Do I have to talk about fear?
So much has already been said

THE STRAW IS TOO LONG, THE AXE IS TOO DULL

a skull floats up from the pond and makes a sound like a gull
        shriek to warn me I have stood here too long   when it dies
back into the water it leaves silence all around and reedstems

            like boiled femurs leaning away   such provocation
      is needed to pull a man open to expose his earthmeat
anyone can understand a skull even the seeds in my pocket

are cracking awake   I can feel the long scar around my neck
       glowing the dock underneath my feet
melting into rust   god in his inestimable wisdom is on the side

       of the big battalions   instead of my one gashable body he would
   have preferred fifty   now my shoes are soaking through
     now the math seems obvious   blue water plus yellow sun equals

green plants it's almost too simple to speak   I am inconsolable I need
       pondfoam and boxed wine in a coffee mug or soothing
saffron and bay leaves I need to be poured dry instead of this slow

     seeping   it hurts to even think about the leak in my brain
where brackish water trickles in and memory trickles out
      with what do I mend a hole like that   answer me   with what

PHOEBE POWER

Phoebe Power received an Eric Gregory Award from the Society of Authors in 2012 and a Northern Writers' Award in 2014. Her poems have been published in journals and anthologies including *The Rialto*, *Oxford Poetry*, *The White Review* and *Aquanauts* (Sidekick Books, 2017). Phoebe has recently collaborated with other artists on projects including a live version of her pamphlet, *Harp Duet* (Eyewear, 2016), and *Christl*, a video installation involving poetry, visual art and sound. *Shrines of Upper Austria* is her first full collection of poetry. She lives in York.

SHRINES OF UPPER AUSTRIA

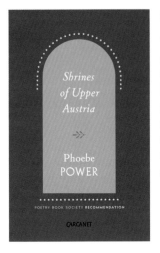

CARCANET | £9.99 | PBS PRICE £7.50

The interface between two languages is the glacial rift that cuts through *Shrines of Upper Austria*. German and English speak side by side, and often break into one another, achieving a giddiness of acoustic effect. Even non-speakers of German, or non-speakers of English, are likely to experience the euphonic excitement of crossing the border, nowhere more in evidence than 'Installation for a New Baby':

> ...The doll of her
> sits forward in a car-seat, up-raised
> polyvinyl queen. *Na ja*, we marker-pen,
> *was kann es schöneres geben*
> *als ein kleines neues Leben?*

This is a richly varied book; though viewed through the focused, bilingual lens of rural Austria, it takes us through the cultural and aesthetic landscapes of the new Europe in which any true sense of home is elusive. Elsewhere, Power has said her concerns are the "spiritual and the kitsch" and this seems aptly to span the book's many bridges. If the latter might be located in Rüdiger von Drachenblut the puppet frog, "...made from blue socks and other scraps, / his polystyrene eyes / coloured green with highlighter" the former is surely located in 'See (2)' – one of many accomplished prose poems in this collection:

> The See looks on. She looks at herself. Because she is the See she can begin to see from the perspective of her liquid centre, her navel, and see all the shores as equidistant from this point.

Shrines of Upper Austria offers a clean European sweep, deftly switching its perspectives from elevated anecdote to the extended lyric-narrative, most notably founded in 'from A Tour of Shrines of Upper Austria' and the six page spread of 'Austrian Murder Case', achieved with an eye for pellucid if disturbing detail:

> ...Inside, right there on the lake path: somebody's feet and hands, cut off.

TIM LIARDET

PHOEBE POWER

This collection is conceived as a collage, a plurality of poems and prose pieces, stories, lyric fragments, and multiple voices which interconnect. Another way to think about this is as a shrine: a gathering of objects, words and images important to someone, both as discrete objects and as a composition. Part of this book is about finding and documenting other people's shrines in a compassionate and joyful way. These constructions might be the religious shrines marking the paths of rural Austria, but could equally include a school student's frog-puppet made out of socks, or a makeshift grave for a pair of goats. The work is also a gathering of pieces into my own scrapbook (or shrine?), in the interest of generating provocative juxtapositions.

I began this book while living in Austria in 2016. As I became immersed in the culture and environment around me, I felt a greater connection to the story of my Austrian grandmother, Christl, who moved to the UK in the wake of the Second World War. In the latter half of the collection, Christl's voice enters the text and becomes an important locus for its ideas. In this way I want to suggest a decentering of the authorial voice, inviting the possibility of dialogue or a duet. The European and British political situations of the time of writing altered my perspective on Christl's status as a displaced person, and on my own as someone able to move freely around Europe. Living in a land whose cultural identity is shaped by long snowy winters also had an effect on how I approached ideas around climate change.

PHOEBE RECOMMENDS

Vahni Capildeo, *Measures of Expatriation* (Carcanet); Anne Carson, *Float* (Cape); Kayo Chingonyi, *Kumukanda* (Chatto & Windus); Matthew and Michael Dickman, *Brother* (Faber); Ruby Robinson, *Every Little Sound* (Liverpool University Press); Melissa Lee-Houghton, *Sunshine* (Penned in the Margins); Caitríona O'Reilly, *Geis* (Bloodaxe); Ahren Warner, *Hello. Your promise has been extracted* (Bloodaxe).

RECOMMENDATION

children running
verging the dark
world of tree and linelessness

Image Credit: Debby Akam, Michael
Hedges, Gary Power and Phoebe Power

STOP 3: ECK 9

this one's for mothers,
all dead and dying mothers.

mary's in a frame there
her dress pulled back to show
her grey and red heart
pierced with a knife and lilies.

jesus too with his bared heart.
and a monk holding a baby
on his arm like a father.

in a frame's a worried mother
kissing the hand of a child in bed.

and a sewn tea-cloth, black thread
on grey-white linen:
Wenn du noch eine Mutter hast,
Danke Gott und sei zufrieden,
Nicht jeden auf der Erderund
Ist dieses höhe Glück beschieden

ROBIN ROBERTSON

Robin Robertson was brought up on the North-East
coast of Scotland and now lives in London. A Fellow
of the Royal Society of Literature, he has published
five collections of poetry and has received a number
of honours, including the Petrarca-Preis, the E.M.
Forster Award from the American Academy of Arts
and Letters and all three Forward Prizes. His selected
poems, *Sailing the Forest*, was published in 2014.

THE LONG TAKE

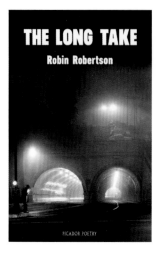

PICADOR | £14.99 | PBS PRICE £11.25

As it moves from New York to Los Angeles to San Francisco between the years 1946 and 1953, and as it breaks between fragmented illuminations and longer takes, Robin Robertson's epic two hundred and fifty page poem achieves the uninterrupted fluency with which Sokurov's single tracking shot followed the French marquis through the seemingly infinite rooms of the State Hermitage Museum. The poem follows the fortunes of Walker, a D-Day veteran with post-traumatic stress disorder, who in his attempts to adjust to a broken world is at times reminiscent of the woebegone Freddie Quell in Paul Thomas Anderson's movie *The Master*. The poem is cinematic at core. As if to emphasize the constricted point of view of the third person lens, there is a sense that Robertson's camera often sits behind the back of Walker as the gigantic American cities swell and rise all around him, while the syntactical movement of the poem itself has a way of generating its own weird, electronic soundtrack as it does so:

> the fabled, smoking ruin, the new towers rising
> through the blue,
> the ranked array of ivory and gold, the glint,
> the glamour of buried light
> as the world turned round it
> very slowly
> this autumn morning, all amazed.

We have come to expect the muscular diction of Robertson's lyrics but *The Long Take* is a major, often disturbing work of extension and amplification, whose principal achievement in the history of the long poem, though it takes breaths between its transitions, rather like the cities in the forties and fifties it inhabits, never actually pauses:

> a river of hats
> following a current, streaming round obstacles
> then re-forming: gray and brown and black.
> It came to him then.
> You can never step into the same city twice.

TIM LIARDET

ROBIN ROBERTSON

Let me be the first to point out that, at over 200 pages, this book does – if nothing else – live up to its title. Through accident more than ambition, I found myself writing a long-form narrative, with characters and dialogue: a fiction set in real places and recounting some real events – though all of it filtered through film or the imagination. I found its shape capacious enough to allow many recurring interests – the pitching of the human against the environment, the fragility of desire and happiness, the abrupt dislocation of violence, the onslaught of age, the long shadows of guilt and shame, the landscape of loss.

I've tried to unpick the lure of cities – those treasuries of glamour and harm, opportunity and loneliness – but never found the right tools. My key to the city turned out to be film, specifically the noir films I've been watching all my life. This gave me the distance and mise-en-scène I needed: the American metropolis where refugee European directors and cinematographers made art from anxiety, where German Expressionism met the American Dream.

The central figure is an ex-soldier from Nova Scotia, unable to return to his island home: deracinated and deranged from the war in Europe, desperate for refuge and repair. The post-war cities of America – New York, Los Angeles, San Francisco – offer up a series of beautiful, brittle illusions, but this is a country morally fractured by racial and economic division, by endemic corruption and crime. This was the time of McCarthy, HUAC, the Cold War, and the beginning of what we're used to now: political paranoia and misinformation, catastrophic foreign policy, and a Nativist domestic climate that has regressed to circling the wagons and shooting the Indians.

This book is not just about war, though – or cities, or America – but more about the balms and barbs of memory, about the frightening slippage and collapse of time and place: a human story of someone trying to recover from trauma, trying to find a way home – to get back to kindness; back to himself.

Night.

The city's gone.
In its place, this gray stone maze, this
locked geometry of shadows, blind and black

Image Credit: Hill Street Tunnels in the fog
Photo: Howard Maxwell, *Los Angeles Times*

1946

Manhattan's twin, her strange, beguiling sister, Coney,
best visited at night, rising up from the sea
ablaze, calling men and women down
toward their dreams and terrors, the white fire
of electricity and light, the chance – in the plummet
of the roller-coaster, the dark-ride, the Wonder Wheel –
for them to hold each other, quickly, somewhere out of sight.

Looka! Looka! Looka! Get your tickets here!
Don't hold back, boys and girls! The ride of your life!

Evenings still hot, but a breeze off the sea
and the smell of French fries, candy, girls' perfume.
The lights are so beautiful, and he picks out a rhythm
in the screams and laughter, the rumble
of the rides, the metal's screeling, through the hundred
different fairground tunes, the thousand calls and shouts,
the noise of America at play
with the crush of the Atlantic
breaking under the boardwalk,
steady and slow.
To be young, and *in this world*. Alive!

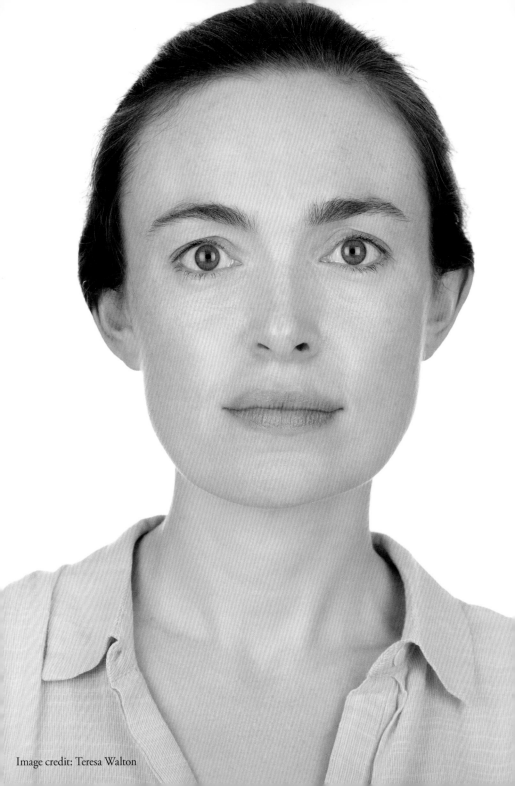

HANNAH SULLIVAN

Hannah Sullivan lives in London and teaches modern English Literature at New College, Oxford. After reading Classics as an undergraduate, she received a PhD in English from Harvard in 2008 and taught at Stanford University in California for three years. Her first published poem appeared in *P.N. Review* in 1998 and so this debut has had a long genesis. Her academic book *The Work of Revision* was, in fact, a study of the complicated and indirect ways in which writers draft and revise. She is currently writing a book on free verse, funded by a Philip Leverhulme Prize.

THREE POEMS

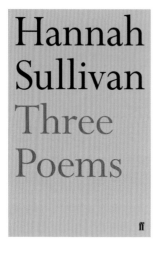

FABER | £10.99 | PBS PRICE £8.25

The three poems that comprise this book, written in the long shadow of *Four Quartets*, are allowed thirteen, twenty two and nineteen pages respectively and this kind of focus and ambition sets it at a distance from the sort of occasional poetry that characterises many debut collections. 'You, Very Young in New York', 'Until Time' and 'The Sandpit After Rain' are unashamedly large-scale, made of multiple movements, shifts in melody and sparks of ideation. Though each poem goes through countless formal variations, from *terza rima*, to couplet, to sonnet, to blank verse and *vers libre* – all of which often incorporate shiny nuggets of rhyme and assonance – it is one music that is heard. The three poems nod hugely and gratefully to the modernist giants, but the voice is as fresh and *au courant* as it can get:

> As the bartenders figure out the winter cocktail lists, telling each other
> That Cynar, grapefruit bitters, and a small-batch Mezcal will
> Be trending in the new year, even though guests are still going to be wanting
> Negronis at weddings, gin and tonics on first dates, Manhattans before
> Moving upstairs, away from the camera phones, on illicit business . . .

Three Poems travels great distances. The poems progress from New York to California, from subsumed lyric to an autobiographical intensity, wading waist-deep in their own philosophical concerns. 'The Sandpit After Rain' acts as centre of gravity and as coda, by some measure the most personal sequence of the book, confronting childbirth and the death of a father as if they are inextricably linked:

> The baby did not look like my father at all,
> But there was a resemblance:
> Our slight awkwardness with each other.

HANNAH SULLIVAN

When I was 21, I went to study for a year in the United States. On my application, I said that I wanted to write poems. But once I arrived the kind of poems I had been writing seemed instantly antiquated – formal, stiff, slight things. And what I liked to read was prose: essays, social satire, novels about business and politics. I ended up staying abroad for ten years, on and off, and I did not write very many poems. Faced by the shapely simplicity of a well-made lyric poem, or a single blank page, I seemed to have nothing to say.

It was only after moving back to England in 2012 that I began again. I wrote the opening of 'You, Very Young in New York' on a wet Sunday night in Oxford, surrounded by marking, ignoring an unwritten lecture, in a mood of wryly melancholic longing for an American life that was starting to seem as if it had happened to someone else. Then I continued to write more "pieces"; at first they felt like alternatives. It took a few months to see that there might be a whole that was more tonally varied, more perspectively complete than the parts. Suddenly my aim wasn't to write a "poem" but a kind of essay in verse.

By a great stroke of luck, I was able to publish this potentially unpublishable hybrid quite quickly in *Areté* magazine, which was having a themed New York issue. Once it appeared, I felt I'd finally discovered a form I could work in or, at least, contend with. The second poem in my book is more philosophical: an essay on repetition and history. The third is a memoir about the death of my father and birth of my first child.

HANNAH RECOMMENDS

2017 has been a rich year. I've especially enjoyed: Emily Berry, *Stranger, Baby* (Faber); Leontia Flynn, *The Radio* (Cape); Jorie Graham, *Fast* (Carcanet); Ishion Hutchinson, *House of Lords and Commons* (Faber); Laura Kasischke, *Where Now: New and Selected Poems* (Copper Canyon Press); Roddy Lumsden, *So Glad I'm Me* (Bloodaxe).

RECOMMENDATION

Image credit: Jo Hume

REPEAT UNTIL TIME

I. I

The picked mosquito bites scab over, resin sap.
The bites are as itchy as ever, and the anaesthetic river
Still concentrates its cold, but the ankles are different this summer,
Less lean, veinier, slower in the river.
Other old women step delicately into the same floodwater,
But the river is different without the nesting moorhens,
And magpies hovering by their uncracked eggs.

There is no stepping twice in same or different rivers.
Nor would anyone step once if she hadn't first shivered,
Toes spooning in the mud, watching an older sister
Striding through grasses, imperiously batting off butterflies.

The river cracks, slides on, a parquet floor for hens.
Clouds filter sea, snow hollows flint, March brings new rains.

LAURIE DUGGAN

Laurie Duggan moved from Australia to Faversham, Kent, in 2006. His most recent books are *No particular place to go* (Bristol: Shearsman Books, 2017) and a reissue of his first two books as *East and Under the Weather* (Sydney: Puncher & Wattman, 2014).

SELECTED POEMS 1971-2017

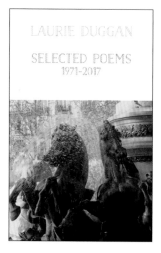

SHEARSMAN | £14.95 | PBS PRICE £11.22

The scope of Laurie Duggan's work, in this generous *Selected Poems*, testifies to an ongoing engagement with an international postmodernist poetics from 1971 to the present. Here we have seven sections, some drawn from longer sequences, and others grouped by periods lasting roughly a decade. The primacy of collage – or bricolage of places, objects and voice – sustains itself here across thirty-five years' worth of poems. The local, which is at times his native Australia or the UK where he now lives, is defamiliarised, abstracted, and returned to the reader as an event of imagination as much as a knowable place. It is therefore no surprise to see aesthetics and, indeed, geographies link through their engagement with other surfaces from art and literature: painting, music, film.

A half-remembered line forms the title of an early poem, 'They can't take that away from me'. Mapping memory against recollection, Duggan invokes the solitary figures of Edward Hopper and ideas of testimony through Charles Reznikoff. The poem is fascinated by marking the specificity of time (the date and hour is invoked precisely) but simultaneously probes what it means to forget.

> Everything passes into history
> The axe falls & the trunk splits
> steam floats away from the tea cup
> Only shape affects us unpredictably
> – there's nothing nostalgic
> about cartography –

However, later poems do involve themselves in a cartography of nostalgia, sometimes with humorous effect. 'A salute to the Cambridge Marxists' might be a tongue-in-cheek reference to fissures in the avant-garde and the poems that follow invoke the poet and publisher Jonathan Williams as well as poet and bookseller Alan Halsey. Later, there is a wistful elegy for the poet Lee Harwood. These more recent poems, in particular the 'Allotment Poems', speak to an easing of modernist poetics and a paring down of the line that feels almost lyrical. Readers familiar with Duggan's work as well as newcomers will find here a seminal contemporary poetic voice of formidable style and range.

SANDEEP PARMAR

SELECTORS' COMMENT

BLUE HILLS 44

So much of a city
is light on stonework, woodwork;
demolition turns us into archaeologists
using the maps;
                    memory,
a particular daub of colour
there, to the right,
of that mountain down the street.

BLUE HILLS 59

all night long

rain, distant

lightning, fires

rumoured

about the city

LULJETA LLESHANAKU

Luljeta Lleshanaku was born in Elbasan, Albania in 1968. Under Enver Hoxha's Stalinist dictatorship, she grew up under house arrest. After the collapse of the regime in the early 1990s she was able to study at the University of Tirana and later attended the MFA Program at Warren Wilson College, USA. She currently works as a research director at the Institute of Studies of Communist Genocide in Albania. She has published seven books of poetry in Albanian and Bloodaxe published her first UK edition, *Haywire: New & Selected Poems* in 2011. She has won several prestigious awards for her poetry, including PEN Albania 2016.

NEGATIVE SPACE

TRANSLATED BY ANI GJIKA

LULJETA LLESHANAKU

NEGATIVE SPACE

TRANSLATED BY ANI GJIKA

BLOODAXE | £12.00 | PBS PRICE £9.00

The Albanian poet Luljeta Lleshanaku's *Negative Space* is her second book in the UK, although New Directions in the US has been publishing her since 2002. Born in 1968 and regarded as the leading poet of her generation, Lleshanaku is powerfully translated here by Ani Gjika. The book begins with a long poem voiced for the Antarctic explorer Frank Wild, Shackleton's right hand man. It is full of vigour and offers a spare yet vivid, almost cinematic, conjuration of Wild's life, which must serve as a kind of analogy to her own. From there she moves through a range of dramatized characters before the first person singular takes over. Her eye is hungry, her sense of detail quite dazzling at times. Most importantly she presents the reader with a believable version of the world. It is as she says in 'Inside a Suitcase':

> my own skin turning into a suitcase,
> packed full with things, as if relocating to another life:
> cotton things, synthetic things, truths, alibis, objects and shadows,
> without the terror of the rattling emptiness.

These are simply things in themselves, a gathering of notable fragments mixing materials with ideas in the most natural way as a tumbling list. She doesn't do anything fancy technically or rhetorically. She speaks straight: it is just that the straight speech is subtle (as is the translation) and puts its fingers on the wounds of the world.

I also enjoyed Karen Leeder's translations of Ulrike Almut Sandig, in *Thick of It* (Seagull). Sandig's poems move with delicacy and sharpness between the objects of the real world and hints of what threatens them. Also Simon Smith's fresh look at Catullus in *The Books of Catullus* (Carcanet) a modern colloquial reading, vivid, edgy, fun, standing at an angle to the straight respectful lyric but rejuvenating it.

GEORGE SZIRTES

THE UNKNOWN

When a child is born, we name it after an ancestor,
and so the recycling continues. Not out of nostalgia,
but from our fear of the unknown.

With a suitcase full of clothes, a few icons, a knife with a shiny blade,
the immigrant brought along names of places he came from
and the places he claimed he named New Jersey, New Mexico,
        Jericho,
New York and Manchester.

The same condition for the unknown above us:
we named planets and stars after capricious, vengeful gods –
Mars, Jupiter, Saturn, Venus, Centaur –
as if making a shield against the cosmos.

Names leap ahead like hunting hounds,
with the belief they clear the road
of the journey's unexpected obstructions.
And we call 'destiny' our common unknown,
a genderless, unconjugated, unspecified name.
Its authority hangs on one shoulder
like the tunic of a Roman senator
leaving only one arm bare and free.

LULJETA LLESHANAKU

RAMONA HERDMAN

After studying creative writing at UEA, Ramona Herdman had a first collection published and a poem in that year's Forward anthology, followed by several blank years of not writing at all. Since 2009, however, she has had poems widely accepted in magazines and anthologies. She lives in Norwich and is a committee member for Café Writers. She won the Poetry Society's Hamish Canham Prize in 2017. She tweets occasionally @ramonaherdman.

BOTTLE

HAPPENSTANCE | £5.00

In *Bottle*, Ramona Herdman presents a clear-eyed account of alcoholism: its snares, its siren calls, its abject downfalls. It is a moving testimony to a long struggle, and a journey towards a tentative reconciliation with a father-figure who suffered from the same condition.

Herdman takes two approaches to the subject: one metaphorical, one anecdotal. The former yields poems such as 'From "The Drunk Circus"', in which trapeze artists represent high levels of risk and surrender:

> you hold each other   up
> with your berserk   belief.

The earthbound aspect comes to the fore in part three of the poem, 'Freaks', in which we are introduced to "the woman bearded with vomit, / the high-heeled twins conjoined / by love and stagger". In the poem 'My Name is Legion: For We Are Many', we are presented with the parable of Christ and "the man of unclean spirit ...dwelling among the tombs" who is possessed by devils; an act of exorcism then casts out the devils into the bodies of swine. For Herdman, possession takes on the form of a disease, which therefore includes the idea of social contagion, the "clean" versus the "unclean" and the social barriers arising from mistrust or disgust.

Among the moving poems to her father, she describes the desire to "reach through his ribs / and pull out the bloody trouble, treacle / mucus", in a similar act of miraculous salvation. A drinker himself, alcohol is at once a cause of separation and a fatal bonding agent, something they share:

> It's only the thought of your life that scares me.
> But if there were an afterlife I'd meet you there, happy hour.
>
> - 'Two Death in The Afternoons, Please'

These poems are testament to Herdman's openness and courage.

A.B. JACKSON

HE'S IN HIS ALTITUDES

The sun's in his eyes.
He's sniffed the barmaid's apron.
He's been bitten by the tavern bitch.
He's on a date with John Barleycorn.
He's got a piece of bread and cheese in the attic.
He's a couple of chapters into the novel.
He's all mops and brooms.
He's moist around the edges.
He's iced to the eyebrows.
His teeth have caught cold.
He's lit up like a church window.
His breath's strong enough to carry coal.
He's bowing to the bottle.
He's bearing his blushing honours thick upon him.
It's starlight with him.
He's among the philistines.
He's been to Olympus and now he's in Liquor Pond.
He's blind as a boiled owl, his head full of bees.
He's sober as a judge on a Friday.
He's bar-kissing.
He's lapping in the gutter.
He's laughing at the carpet.
He's keeping his sails up, beating on against an ale-head wind.
He's swallowed a hare.
He's keg-legged.
There's a brick in his hat.
He's Adam's apple up.
He's in bed with his boots on

NATURAL PHENOMENA
MERYL PUGH

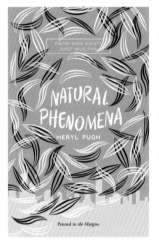

PENNED IN THE MARGINS | £9.99 | PBS £7.50

The poems in Meryl Pugh's first collection, *Natural Phenomena*, have a beguiling musicality. As I read the book, I was struck by the timbre of the words; the ways in which sound carries meaning even when referential meaning is elusive. That is not to say that these are murky or wilfully obscure poems but rather that the poet is adept in employing a range of effects particular to poetic form so that nothing in the poem is accidental and the whole contributes to a heady atmosphere that washes over you as you read. What is especially refreshing when this approach is wedded to a perspective as assured and integrated as Pugh's is that a number of subtle resonances emerge as the book unfolds:

Radio station, warm in the ears, cream tiles
blue-lit underpass.

- '5 nights'

Let me see you put your hands in the air
there is laughter
cheering   hand-clapping and faint
orange   faint grey   clearing
to blue

- 'Transit'

Such gestures towards and breakings away from sonic patterns abound in the book and make for a compelling point of ingress to the book's central project: the attempt to set human life in a wider context and, as a consequence, invite questions about how we respond to the natural world and its dwindling resources which fuel so much of what we think of as technological advancement. The book seems to be saying "get over yourself", responding to a particular world view that centres human life by showing us how expansive our world truly is.

KAYO CHINGONYI

KAYO CHINGONYI

Kayo Chingonyi is a fellow of the Complete Works programme for diversity and quality in British Poetry and the author of two pamphlets, *Some Bright Elegance* (Salt, 2012) and *The Colour of James Brown's Scream* (Akashic, 2016). Kayo has been invited to read from his work around the world and his poems have been translated into Spanish, German, and Swedish. He was awarded the 2012 Geoffrey Dearmer Prize and served as Associate Poet at the Institute of Contemporary Arts from Autumn 2015 to Spring 2016. His first full-length collection, *Kumukanda*, was published by Chatto & Windus.

GUEST SELECTOR

OTHER NEW BOOKS

THICK OF IT: ULRIKE ALMUT SANDIG
TRANSLATED BY KAREN LEEDER

The German poet Ulrike Almut Sandig began her poetic career pasting poems onto lamp posts in Leipzig. Her poems are free "slender shadows" crossing geographies and time. Beautifully crafted and achingly modern, this collection journeys through language and the imagination "into the thicket" of words and the world. Restless and precarious, *Thick of It* is a truly mesmerising collection, full of energy and urgency.

SEAGULL BOOKS | £12.99 | PBS PRICE £9.75

ASYLUM: SEAN BORODALE

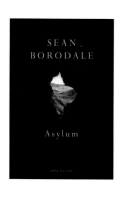

This collection focuses upon what lies beneath our feet – deeply beneath. Rock and soil, graves, caves and mines are the subjects of Borodale's evocative poems. With the attitude of a geologist and archaeologist the poet excavates buried remains and subterranean microcosms, uncovering a sense of enormity in the formations of stalactites, the laying down of sediments, and the ceaseless processes of decay.

JONATHAN CAPE | £10.00 | PBS PRICE £7.50

SPOILS: JAMES BROOKES

Spoils by James Brookes is a collection exploring the contemporary relevance of folklore and history in the context of the everyday through darkly avant-garde imagery and rich, dense language that retains a distinctly modern voice. Jumping off from classical reference points, the book delves into present-day frustrations in a narrative voice steeped in bitter irony and an awareness of a world stacked against the everyman.

OFFORD ROAD | £12.00 (HB) | PBS PRICE £9.00

OTHER NEW BOOKS

ASSEMBLY LINES: JANE COMMANE

Assembly Lines is a pragmatic love song to the post-industrial town. Described as presenting a "new Midlands realism" this is a book that casts a pragmatic gaze on the power of romanticism in a world where many are left behind. Commane's debut collection paints a vital, loving portrait of very recognisable modern Britain in a voice that is clear, calm and distinct. An instant classic.

BLOODAXE | £9.95 | PBS PRICE £7.47

CITY OF BONES: KWAME DAWES

Kwame Dawes' latest poetry collection (his twentieth) is a moving testament from a remarkable poet. Dawes uses a range of voices to powerful effect, absorbing and re-telling the stories of the African diaspora, exploring the history and legacy of slavery and the challenges facing many Americans today. This collection is bold, moving, thoughtful and celebratory in equal parts. And at over 250 pages, it is a huge body of work demanding to be returned to and read again and again.

PEEPAL TREE | £12.99 | PBS PRICE £9.75

LUCK IS THE HOOK: IMTIAZ DHARKER

Luck is the Hook is Imtiaz Dharker's sixth collection published by Bloodaxe Books. With poems that awaken all your senses, this collection explores themes of chance, travel and changes in the passing of time. The title of the collection appears in the five page poem 'This Tide of Humber' which was commissioned by BBC Strong Language Festival and celebrates the river Humber and Hull's unique sense of place as 2017's UK City of Culture.

BLOODAXE | £12.00 | PBS PRICE £9.00

OTHER NEW BOOKS

BLOTTER: OLI HAZZARD

Five formally various and experimental sequences which unpick the inadequacy of words: "the weather / vanishing behind the words for it // pip pip". Hazzard questions the linearity of poetry, language and "the fiction / of a person". Fragmentary and fluid, these poems converge and collide: "There is some connection. / We have it. No, wait. / They have it. No, wait. / No." Full of erasures, found poems and blotting out, this is daring, dexterous and innovative: " Steel yourself / for an act of originality".

CARCANET | £9.99 | PBS PRICE £7.50

URN AND DRUM: LILA MATSUMOTO

These aphoristic and comic poems are accompanied by a series of pencil drawings, bizarre photographs and carvings which tell their own stories. Matsumoto revels in the absurdity of the everyday and delights in the quirky linguistic joy of "smooshable foodstuffs", "sincere pickles" and "self-help muesli". Witty poems about finding a "vintage pancake in the crevice between refrigerator and wall" are counterbalanced by flashes of sublime beauty: "outside the wild mind: / evening's keening."

SHEARSMAN | £9.95 | PBS PRICE £7.47

BLACK SUN: TOBY MARTINEZ DE LAS RIVAS

Playful and sincere, obtuse and profound, *Black Sun* draws upon a diaspora of linguistic and textual strands – including Spanish, Greek and religious references – to form an extremely effective collection. The mundane and the metaphysical, past and present, mind and place, death, memory and imagination become a tightly-woven whole. Reading *Black Sun* is like dropping into a lyrical otherworld. Rising above all is the black sun itself, appearing as a sinister literal image, ringed with strange solar flares of verse.

FABER | £10.99 | PBS PRICE £8.25

OTHER NEW BOOKS

SHORTENING THE CANDLE'S WICK: LY SEPPEL & ANDRES EHIN | TRANSLATED BY ILMAR LEHTPERE

A poetic dialogue between two of Estonia's most distinguished poets, husband and wife Andres Ehin and Ly Seppel. Their still and watchful poems give voice to a "worldwide quietening" and echo within one another: "it is ourselves we hear". Sometimes epic, sometimes cryptic, these poems are sorrowful forested mindscapes: "The inner forest / within veins empty of blood". Each scene is filled with light, memory, "the soft shimmer of meaning" and hints of Estonia's darker past.

LITTLE ISLAND PRESS | £12.99 HB | PBS PRICE £9.75

DON'T CALL US DEAD: DANEZ SMITH

In the poem, 'dear white america', Smith suggests a figure of the nation with "joints brittle & dragging a ripped gown through Oakland". This moral and physical decrepitude embodies the poet's fatigue with a nation whose white institutions mete out violence upon racial others with casual abandon. Graphic sex forms a refuge against routine shootings but AIDS extends the violence. Both fearful and fearless, Smith says he leaves "revenge hopelessly to God", but this collection serves as a relentless call for change and resistance.

CHATTO & WINDUS | £10.99 | PBS PRICE £8.25

WAY MORE THAN LUCK: BEN WILKINSON

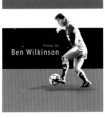

This is a powerful debut collection split into three sections. In the first, experiences with depression and its ever looming nature are revealed along with learning to combat this through running. The middle section then cleverly brings to life the inner characters of a number of Liverpool football legends in lyrical praise for the beautiful game. The final section brings us back, with a bump and occasional wry smile, to the real world.

SEREN | £9.99 | PBS PRICE £7.50

PAMPHLETS

This deftly composed poem sequence, paired with Anna Vaivare's vibrant illustrations, moves through the life of a female artist during the early part of the twentieth century. Beginning from age nine, towards and past the point where the unnamed artist has a child of her own, *Now You Can Look* has a sharp, immediate quality which pulls you firmly into a life which both did and did not exist – vanished, imagined, or perhaps something else.

THE   EMMA   PRESS | £10.00 |

──────── ALL OF THE SPACES: MARIA ISAKOVA BENNETT ────────

Bennett explores the absence in "gestures of presence", the "solace" of the white space between words and the solitary beauty of a moment spent watching hail. At times fractured and experimental, others pliant and fluid, each stanza is exquisitely sculpted. Nostalgia pervades too in childhood memories which are both warm and bleak, reminding us of those poignant "spaces" between people, past and present, reality and memory.

EYEWEAR   PUBLISHING | £6.00 |

──────── THUS THE BLUE HOUR COMES: TESS JOLLY ────────

A half-awake dream state governs Tess Jolly's unusual and unsettling pamphlet. The sequence is suffused with night terrors, moon-dreams, pre-dawn hallucinations and the evocative landscape of dark forests. Folk terror and superstition infiltrate each verse, the poet drawing attention to a series of layers – skins, surfaces and shadows – and then transforming them, imbuing them with strange qualities, conjuring and dissolving their illusions.

INDIGO DREAMS PUBLISHING | £6.00 |

PAMPHLETS

A compelling and carefully curated selection of poems from the T.S. Eliot shortlisted Anglo-Iranian poet Mimi Khalvati. Spanning six previous collections, this compact *Very Selected* captures the tender beauty and despair of Khalvati's poetry. Formally accomplished and emotionally rich, these poems range through villanelles to traditional Persian *ghazals* which urge us to see the world anew: "How do you see this tree? Is it really green?"

SMITH | DOORSTOP | £7.50 |

CALDBECK: JENNY PAGDIN

Jenny Pagdin's meditation on postnatal depression and psychosis commences and concludes with definitions of love and hope both poetic and clinical. Between these bookends lies a devastating and tightly formed sequence chronicling the process of onset, diagnosis and recovery. Pagdin lingers no more than is necessary at any one stage, delivering concise and lucid glimpses into mental states, times and places. A compelling and vital portrait.

EYEWEAR PUBLISHING | £6.00 |

SOMEWHERE BETWEEN ROSE AND BLACK: CLAIRE WALKER

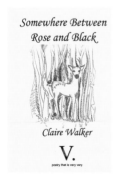

Claire Walker's second pamphlet is inspired by her Great Aunt Mollie's diary. We journey through the pages as she explores the wintry outdoors and describes colours, the time of day and sounds in a way that makes us feel as though we are right by her side. Her portraits of plants and animals give a real earthiness to these poems and provide images that will stay with you long after reading.

V. PRESS | £6.50 |

PBS PRESENTS

STANZA POETRY FESTIVAL LECTURE
SPONSORED BY THE POETRY BOOK SOCIETY

The Poetry Book Society is honoured to sponsor the StAnza Lecture by PBS Summer Choice Sinéad Morrissey. StAnza Festival is one of the top poetry festivals in the UK, based in St Andrews. Sinéad's lecture will explore ideas of persona, trauma and authenticity in contemporary poetry.

8th March | 3.30pm | The Town Hall | St Andrews | £4.50

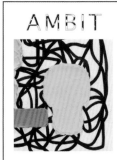

SPRING LISTINGS

NEW BOOKS

AUTHOR	TITLE	PUBLISHER	RRP
Kaveh Akbar	Calling a Wolf a Wolf	Penguin	£9.99
Ken Bolton	Species of Spaces	Shearsman Books	£9.95
Danielle Boodoo-Fortuné	Doe Songs	Peepal Tree Press	£8.99
Sean Borodale	Aslyum	Jonathan Cape	£10.00
James Brookes	Spoils	Offord Road Books	£12.00
Sophie Collins	Who Is Mary Sue?	Penguin Books	£8.99
Francis Combes	If the Symptoms Persist	Smokestack Books	£8.99
Jane Commane	Assembly Lines	Bloodaxe Books	£9.95
Wendy Cope	Anecdotal Evidence	Faber & Faber	£10.99
Kwame Dawes	City of Bones	Peepal Tree Press	£12.99
Ned Denny	Unearthly Toys	Carcanet Press	£12.99
Imtiaz Dharker	Luck Is the Hook	Bloodaxe Books	£12.00
Laurie Duggan	Selected Poems 1971-2017	Shearsman Books	£14.95
Martin Figura	Whistle	Cinnamon Press	£8.99
Anne Fitzgerald	Vacant Possession	Salmon Poetry	£12.00
Nigel Forde	Trace Elements	Valley Press	£10.99
Andrew Geary	Shoal of Powan	Rockingham Press	£9.99
Harry Gilonis	Rough Breathing: Selected Poems	Carcanet Press	£12.99
Clive Gresswell	Jargon Busters	Knives Forks Spoons	£8.00
Lucy Hamilton	Of Heads and Hearts	Shearsman Books	£9.95
Oli Hazzard	Blotter	Carcanet Press	£9.99
Paul Henry	The Glass Aisle	Seren	£9.99
Hamish Ironside	Three Blue Beans	IRON Press	£7.00
Igor Kholin	Kholin 66	Ugly Duckling Presse	£14.00
Arno Kramer	Morningrustle	Salmon Poetry	£12.00
Toby Martinez de las Rivas	Black Sun	Faber & Faber	£10.99
Lila Matsumoto	Urn and Drum	Shearsman Books	£9.95
Liam McCormick	BEAST	Burning Eye Books	£9.99
David McLoghlin	Santiago Sketches	Salmon Poetry	£12.00
Esther Morgan	The Wound Register	Bloodaxe Books	£9.95
Leanne O'Sullivan	A Quarter of an Hour	Bloodaxe Books	£9.95
Bobby Parker	Working Class Voodoo	Offord Road Books	£10.00
Abigail Parry	Jinx	Bloodaxe Books	£9.95
Frederick Pollack	Landscape with Mutant	Smokestack Books	£8.99
Phoebe Power	Shrines of Upper Austria	Carcanet Press	£9.99
J.H. Prynne	The Oval Window	Bloodaxe Books	£12.00
Meryl Pugh	Natural Phenomena	Penned in the Margins	£9.99
Susan Richardson	Words the Turtle Taught Me	Cinnamon Press	£8.99
Elizabeth Rimmer	Haggards	Red Squirrel Press	£8.99
Robin Robertson	The Long Take	Picador	£14.99
Ian Seed	New York Hotel	Shearsman Books	£9.95
Josh Seigal	Advice to a Young Skydiver	Burning Eye Books	£9.99
Danez Smith	Don't Call Us Dead	Chatto & Windus	£10.99
Hannah Sullivan	Three Poems	Faber & Faber	£10.99
James Sutherland-Smith	The River and the Black Cat	Shearsman Books	£9.95
Robin Thomas	Momentary Turmoil	Cinnamon Press	£8.99
Eleni Vakalo (Trans. Karen Emmerich)	Before Lyricism	Ugly Duckling Presse	£15.00
Ben Wilkinson	Way More Than Luck	Seren	£9.99
Luke Wright	Frankie Vah	Penned in the Margins	£9.99

SPRING LISTINGS

TRANSLATIONS

AUTHOR	TITLE	PUBLISHER	RRP
Sherko Bekas (trans. Choman Hardi)	Butterfly Valley	Arc Publications	£10.99
Gaius Valerius Catullus	The Books of Catullus	Carcanet Press	£12.99
Kristiina Ehin (trans. Ilmar Lehtpere)	On the Edge of a Sword	Arc Publications	£9.99
Andres Ehin and Ly Seppel (trans. Ilmar Lehtpere)	Shortening the Candle's Wick	Little Island Press	£12.99
Gerður Kristný (trans. Rory McTurk)	Drápa	Arc Publications	£9.99
Luljeta Lleshanaku	Negative Space	Bloodaxe Books	£12.00
Ulrike Almut Sandig	Thick of It	Seagull Books	£12.99
Abdourahman A. Waberi	Naming the Dawn	Seagull Books	£12.99
Eleni Vakalo (Trans. Karen Emmerich)	Before Lyricism	Ugly Duckling Presse	£15.00

PAMPHLETS

AUTHOR	TITLE	PUBLISHER	RRP
Joel Auterson	Unremember	Bad Betty Press	£5.00
Michael Bartholomew-Biggs	The Man Who Wasn't Ever Here	Wayleave Press	£5.00
Julia Bird	Now You Can Look	The Emma Press	£10.00
D M Black	The Bi-plane and other poems	Mariscat Press	£6.00
James Caruth	Narrow Water	Poetry Salzburg	£7.00
David Greenslade	Objects from the Footcopier	Red Ceilings Press	£7.00
Ramona Herdman	Bottle	HappenStance Press	£5.00
Maria Isakova Bennett	all of the spaces	Eyewear Publishing	£6.00
Tess Jolly	Thus the blue hour comes	Indigo Dreams	£6.00
Mimi Khalvati	Very Selected Poems	Smith|Doorstop	£7.50
Anna Kisby	All the Naked Daughters	Against the Grain	£5.00
Michael Laskey	Very Selected Poems	Smith|Doorstop	£7.50
James McGonigal	Turning Over in a Strange Bed	Mariscat Press	£6.00
Jenny Pagdin	Caldbeck	Eyewear Publishing	£6.00
Stav Poleg	Lights, Camera	Eyewear Publishing	£6.00
Michael Schmidt	Very Selected Poems	Smith | Doorstop	£7.50
Keshia Starrett	Hysterical	Burning Eye Books	£6.99
Deborah Turnbull	Trial By Scar	Eyewear Publishing	£6.00
Simon Turner	Birmingham Jazz Incarnation	The Emma Press	£5.00
Claire Walker	Somewhere Between Rose and Black	V. Press	£6.50
Lois Williams	Like Other Animals	HappenStance Press	£5.00
Patrick Wright	Nullaby	Eyewear Publishing	£6.00
Gareth Writer-Davies	Cry Baby	Indigo Dreams	£6.00
Tim Youngs	Mr	more shoots more leaves	£5.00